THE LITTLE BOOK OF
Good Things!

THE LITTLE BOOK OF
Good Things!

BHAVYA DOSHI

Founder of The Doodle Desk

HAY HOUSE INDIA

New Delhi • London • Sydney
Carlsbad, California • New York City

Hay House Publishers (India) Pvt Ltd
Muskaan Complex, Plot No. 3, B-2, Vasant Kunj, New Delhi – 110070, India

Hay House LLC, P.O. Box 5100, Carlsbad, CA 92018-5100, USA
Hay House UK Ltd, 1st Floor, Crawford Corner, 91-93 Baker Street, London W1U 6QQ, UK
Hay House Australia Publishing Pty Ltd, 18/36 Ralph St., Alexandria NSW 2015, Australia

Email: contact@hayhouse.co.in
Website: www.hayhouse.co.in

ISBN 978-93-6611-120-9 (paperback)

Typeset at Hay House India
by Raghav Khattar

For my beloved father, Dr Dilip Doshi,
and my darling mother, Renuka Doshi,
who now live in heaven.

AUTHOR'S NOTE

It was not very long ago that life made me go through one of the most painful experiences known to humankind—losing both my parents. I was broken beyond words and struggled to build myself again. But art helped me to do so, piece by piece.

I started The Doodle Desk as a medium for self-expression but was astonished to see the impact it had on others. Soon, it turned into a movement for giving hope to others and became the 'art of spreading joy'. Today, it humbles me to see the love The Doodle Desk receives from people across the world. It is this love that pushes me to go above and beyond in my attempt to spread joy. It is this faith that made me want to venture into new spaces and reach new people while serving my existing virtual family.

Upon contemplation about more ways to spread joy, it occurred to me that the gentle and affectionate touch of a loved one has the power to heal even the deepest wounds. This is why I wanted my art and words to be held by people. I wanted them to touch it, to feel it. I wanted them to find the warmth of a loved one in it. Hence, *The Little Book of Good Things!*

This little book of mine is now yours. I have shared my thoughts on different areas of life. I hope they add a little sunshine to your gloomy days and a little warmth to the cold ones. I hope that, as you flip through the pages of this book, you will discover a more positive and stronger version of yourself. I hope that you will love yourself a little more and be kinder to yourself and others.

Lastly, I believe some encounters are too magical to be a mere coincidence. I believe they are conspired into existence by the universe. I hope when you reminisce about such encounters, you think of this book too.

With love,
Bhavya Doshi

OPEN TO RECEIVING
from the Universe!
Love
Money
Job
Travel

Open to receiving from the universe!

You can't get any new emails when your inbox is full. To receive an email, it is important that you first delete the emails you no longer need. And once you do that, nothing can stop you from receiving new emails.

Likewise, in order to receive what you want from the universe, you must be open to receiving them. This would first require you to be crystal clear about your desires. You can do so by writing them down, saying them out loud, creating a vision board, or by doing anything and everything that helps you declare your desires.

Once you have declared your desires, ensure that you have made space for them to enter your life, both literally and metaphorically. If it is a soulmate that you want, ensure that you haven't shut all the doors for love to enter your life. Be open to new experiences and meeting new people. Be open to giving new people a chance.

This concept applies to other areas of our lives as well. It could be a dream job that you wish to attract or a client that you wish to work for. Everything becomes achievable when you make space for it in your life. And once you do that successfully, visualise achieving them with the purest intentions in your heart. This way you will make your life like an empty mailbox that is ready to receive the blessings from the universe.

YOU ARE THE AUTHOR
of your story!

You are the author of your story!

We all are authors, continuously writing the stories of our lives. Every day we wake up to write a new chapter and decide how our life's story will unfold, one chapter at a time. The important thing to remember here is that our story is nothing but a collection of conscious choices that we make. If we consciously choose happiness at every step of our life, then our story will be a happy one. If we fret over the past and over things that we cannot control, our story will not be a happy one.

Live every day as if it will directly have an impact on the story of your life. Be picky about people and things you spend your energy on. Demand happiness and joy from life and be open to receiving it. Leave your past behind and focus just on the present. When you sleep, sleep believing that you are blessed and worthy of doing great things. When you wake up, wake up wanting to make it the best day of your life, no matter what the circumstances are. And before you know it, you will become an award-winning author!

DO WHAT IT
takes!

Do what it takes!

We have always been asked to have a 'Plan B' that we can hold on to if and when our original plan fails. It is always safe to have a backup option and maybe people who recommend it to us wish the best for us. But to truly test our determination when it comes to the pursuit of our goals, we should work on our plan as if it is our only option and be willing to give it all that it needs. If it demands hours of research, we should feed it with research. If it requires knowledge, we should be open to absorbing knowledge. If it needs creativity, we should let our creativity run riot. And if it requires love and positivity, we should keep a tab on the energy we radiate.

So, let's do ourselves a favour and take a note the next time you set a goal. Ask yourself that are you really giving it your 100 per cent? If the answer is a no or a maybe, it is a sign that you need to pull your socks up and become more determined . . . because it is either 100 per cent or nothing!

EVERYDAY IS A
Fresh Start!

Everyday is a fresh start!

Life doesn't end the moment you make a mistake or disappoint someone. It doesn't end when you get heartbroken or fail. It goes on and gives us a new chance every day . . . a new chance to rectify our mistakes, fix our heart, and live life differently.

However, sometimes when things don't work out the way we would want them to, we feel shattered and think of it as the end. We spend so much of our time wishing our life was different that we fail to notice the opportunity we get every single day to bring about this change.

The only method to live life perfectly is the method of trial and error. Don't overcomplicate. Listen to your heart and do what it says without having the fear of making wrong decisions. This is better than making no decisions at all. Don't hesitate from travelling on some wrong paths till you discover the right one.

My dear friend, don't be embarrassed by everything that goes wrong because it will only lead you towards the right. So, let the past remain in the past and let's look forward to a fresh start every day!

HAPPEANESS IS
an inside job!

Happiness is an inside job!

How are you feeling right now? Are you happy where you are, or do you want to be somewhere else? If your answer is the latter, it is time to shake yourself up a little and change your perspective because chances are that you are looking for happiness in the wrong place.

Now you might think what is the right place then? The answer is that the right place is inside you. Yes, it's true. When we give something or someone the power to make us happy, we provide them with the ability to control our lives. It's like letting someone drive your car at a speed they like, put on the songs that they want to listen to, and take you to a destination of their choice. None of us would want that. Similarly, let's stop expecting someone or something to make us happy. Happiness is an inside job that we should work for, sometimes from 9 to 5, and if it requires, even do the overtime.

We must find what makes us happy and do more of that. This will also help us understand ourselves better. A win-win situation, isn't it? Let's never forget that our life is a car that only we should drive, even if we are not the best driver at the time being!

BE LOVE,
be light!

Be love, be light!

There is more to people than meets the eye. Every single person that we cross paths with has a background story that we have no idea about. On the surface, it might seem that everything is fine but only when we look beyond the surface, we will find out that people are just as broken as us. They all have battles that they don't tell anyone about. They all have something that keeps them up at night. They all have challenges to overcome. But what we need to realise is that they all are human beings with complex emotions just like us.

This makes it crucial for all of us to be tender with people and become a source of love and light for them. Love is an energy within us. We assume that it involves liking a person beyond words but it is so much more. Love is when you accept people as they are and you are ready to offer kindness without expecting anything in return. It is selfless energy that is forever giving. To be light for someone means to share the warmth and wisdom that we have within us.

We all have this love and light within us. All we need to do is find it, channel it, and then sprinkle it on everyone we meet!

WHEN ONE FORGIVES
two souls are set free!

When one forgives, two souls are set free!

We meet different kinds of people in our lives and not all of them are kind to us. And sometimes, the actions and words of such people can have a long-lasting effect on us. This could lead to holding on to the hurt for months and years which eventually becomes a grudge. But what we fail to realise is that grudge is a double-edged sword. Not only does it affect the person it is held against, but it also harms the one who harbours it. It fills us up with negative feelings of bitterness, anger, and resentment. These feelings dim the light of life within us.

Thus, we must free ourselves from all grudges by forgiving people and letting them go. But how can we do that? We can do so by first acknowledging that the reason why people hurt others is that they are hurt themselves. The relationship we have with others often showcases the relationship we have with ourselves. When people are not happy with themselves, they project their hurt on other people.

So, whenever someone hurts you, remember that the real hurt lies within them and that you are not to be blamed. This realisation is the key to set yourself free and let go of all grudges in your life. This will also make you more empathetic towards such unkind people as you will understand that they didn't know any better. Instead of harbouring any bitter feelings against them, say a silent prayer for them and send them love and light.

Yes, my dear friend, what they did to you was wrong but by holding a grudge, you give them the power to hurt you every day. Remember, that forgiveness is for the brave, and being brave is always a choice.

YOU ARE
full of magic!

You are full of magic!

We have a billion cells in our body. Each cell works in astonishing ways and is as magical as the other. This makes us nothing but a cluster of magic, but the humdrum of life tends to make us forget that. However, it is important that we acknowledge the power we hold within and keep it alive. We must recognise that if we tap into this magic, we can shape the life that we desire. After all, no dream is impossible, if one has a magic wand.

But the important question here is that how can we tap into this magic? It is possible to do so by choosing positive thoughts as thoughts eventually become things. This process of turning thoughts into reality is called *manifestation*. And just like any other skill, the art of manifesting requires time and patience to learn and improve upon. Some of the ways we can do this is by being positive, grateful, and believing that we already have what we want. All this helps to raise our vibrations.

Let's practise this skill, shall we? Let's remind ourselves that the universe is a wish-granting factory, waiting for us to manifest our wishes. Let's assure ourselves that everything that we say or do sends a direct message (yes, a DM) to the universe. And let's keep the worries aside because the universe will never leave us on 'seen'!

EVERYTHING THAT IS REAL
was imagined first!

Everything that is real was imagined first!

The pen we use, the bean bag we sit on, the smartphone we spend hours using, and even this book in your hands—all of them were imagined at some point by their respective creators. Their imagination was the foundation of their realities.

We, too, can use imagination as a tool to manifest the reality we desire. This is where the power of positive imagination comes to play. If we want a car then we should imagine driving one. If we want a new house, we should imagine living in one. If we want a thriving career, we should imagine having one. And if we want a relationship, we should imagine being in one. Imagining what our heart desires will not only brighten our days but will also convince us that our desires are achievable.

That being said, it is impossible to keep ourselves away from negative thoughts and from imagining ourselves in negative situations. But it is completely possible to replace them with positive ones. It is somewhat similar to replacing an empty ink cartridge in a pen with a new one. We do so because the empty ink cartridge no longer adds any value to the pen. Likewise, negative thoughts don't add any value to our lives, and we must replace them with positive thoughts which, in turn, have a positive impact on our lives.

RADIATE

Positivity!

Radiate positivity!

What if you didn't have a body and instead were just a collection of all the words you have ever spoken, jokes you have made, deeds you have done, and the energy that you have emitted in the universe. If this were the case, would you still be loved by the people around you and would they still be drawn towards you and your aura?

If your answer is no or maybe, we can work on the energy you radiate. Because it is this energy that can break or mend hearts, make someone smile or frown, and make this world a better place. So, it is important to become very conscious of the energy you give out in the universe. Make sure it is soothing enough to heal someone's pain, warm enough to comfort a cold heart, and accepting enough to give people the space to be themselves. Think before you say and do something. Know that it will directly affect someone's life and only then choose the words and actions based on the effect you want to have on them.

Radiate positivity and leave some sparkle wherever you go!

BE THE TYPE OF PERSON
you want to meet!

Be the type of person you want to meet!

Growing up means crossing paths with a lot of people. Some become our friends, some become our colleagues, some become mentors, while some become a part of our past. And if we are lucky, some become our future.

Now consider this—if given a chance to meet someone right now, who would it be? Will it be your ex-boss? Will it be your school teacher? Will it be your ex? Or will it be your parents? I am pretty sure that you have a name buzzing in your head right now. Take a moment to think why did you choose this person. Is it because they make you feel like no one else does? Is it because you enjoy their company? Is it because you get to learn something from them every time you meet them? Whatever your reason might be, we can become what draws our attention, i.e., we can become the person we want to meet. It might take time, patience, hard work, and maybe tons of self-love, but we can all get there.

So, if it is the humility of a person that we admire, we can learn how to be humble. If it is their rootedness that we love, we can become rooted. Recognising the reason behind why we want to meet a particular person is the first step to become like them in our own unique way. Here's a fun fact, or let's call it a delightful possibility: Maybe the next person to read this will choose you as the person they want to meet.

LITTLE MORE KINDNESS
little less judgement!

Little more kindness, little less judgement!

Do you ever find yourself being judgemental? If your answer is yes then you are not alone. We have all been there when our inner critique takes over us, while the kindness in us takes a back seat. We are capable of judging strangers, our friends, the government, and even Mondays! Maybe being judgemental is one of the most natural feelings that come to us as human beings, or perhaps, we have been conditioned to be judgemental by society. Whatever the reason might be, it is entirely possible to let go of this feeling/conditioning.

For instance, if you ever get into an argument with a delivery boy and think that he has been rude to you, try to take a step back and look beyond the surface. Instead of forming a quick judgement about him, open yourself to other possibilities as well. Maybe the delivery boy was having a rough day, or maybe he was going through a difficult phase in his personal life, or maybe he was just tired by spending so much time in the sun.

So, if you find yourself being consumed by judgements, remind yourself to be more empathetic. With such constant reminders, kindness will make your heart its permanent residence. Also, let's never forget that we all have wounds we are trying to heal and kindness can work like an ointment, both for us and the people we are kind towards.

THE WAY YOU SPEAK to Yourself matters!

The way you speak to yourself matters!

During our formative years, our parents spent a considerable amount of their time and energy teaching us how to speak to others. They guided us towards an ideal way to speak to our relatives and friends and even them. However, one thing that parents usually don't teach us is how to talk to ourselves.

As humans, we are our biggest critic. All it takes for us to engage in negative self-talk is an unfavourable circumstance. For example, if our love isn't reciprocated in the way we would want, we become critical of ourselves, or if we fail to achieve a goal, we start doubting our skills. We think of ourselves as a failure for something as small as not sticking to a new year's resolution. But we don't have this attitude towards our friends and family members. Every time they fail, we try to lift them up and reassure them. That is precisely how we should treat ourselves too. We should talk to ourselves the way we would speak to someone we admire. This will help us admire ourselves!

So, let's mend our self-judgemental ways and start treating ourselves better by giving positive affirmations. Remind yourself that you are beautiful even on the days when you feel otherwise. Tell yourself that you are a success magnet each time you fail at something. And finally, convince yourself that you are healthy on the days you finish three pizzas in a row! Remember that speaking to ourselves in a positive manner is a skill that we need to learn on our own.

FIND HAPPINESS IN
where you are!

Find happiness in where you are!

Happiness is a state of mind. Thus, a happy person will have happy thoughts while an unhappy person will have not so happy thoughts. However, happy thoughts don't always come to us naturally. Thus, we need to train our mind to think happy thoughts and once we acquire this skill, we will realise that happiness can always be found within. Then we won't have to depend on a person, a job title, or a particular outcome to feel happy as it would simply become a part of our being.

Now you might wonder how you can train your mind to think happy thoughts? it is simpler than you imagine.

1. Learn to take life less seriously. Don't let the words and actions of others get to you.
2. Don't dwell on a bad thought. Instead, actively choose a good thought over a bad one.
3. Change your perspective and try to look at life differently.

Try all of the above exercises and see how your mind gradually learns to think about happier thoughts and witness yourself becoming a happier person!

LIFE IS ABOUT
Creating Yourself!

Life is about creating yourself!

There are two kinds of people you get to meet in your life. The first lot consists of people who are free-flowing like water and can change when the situation demands them to. You look at such people with admiration and their growth inspires you to push the envelope too. The second lot consists of people who always complain about change. They have a hard time seeing people around them grow and often criticise other people when that happens.

The important thing to realise here is that staying the same is a deliberate choice to not become a better version of oneself. This hinders growth and stops us from exploring our fullest potential. But on the other hand, personal growth isn't as easy as it sounds. It asks us to let go of our old beliefs, negative traits, emotional baggage, and childhood trauma. It also requires us to cultivate a sense of purpose, learn to take criticism, and view every challenge as an opportunity.

Remember that to be open to growth is to be open to change. It is a hard choice but once we are open to it, it continuously pushes us to become a better person. We have the power to create ourselves as and when we want to!

STORMS DON'T LAST
Forever!

Storms don't last forever!

There is something very heartbreaking about this world and it is that nothing here lasts forever. Loss is inevitable and everyone has to go through it at some point in their lives. These losses give us emotional pain and make us wonder if this period of grief will ever be over and if we will ever be able to experience joy again.

The truth is that time is the ultimate healer. It will act as an ointment for your wounds. And with time, getting up in the morning won't be a struggle for you anymore. It will teach you to come to terms with your loss, no matter how bad it might seem right now.

Till then, be patient and hopeful when you find yourself stuck in a storm. Look for ways to heal your pain. It is also important to feel your feelings and decipher what they are trying to teach you. But in the end, ALWAYS keep your face towards the sunshine because the sun is going to rise again very soon!

DECISIONS DETERMINE
Destiny!

Decisions determine destiny!

We have been told that destiny is a predetermined course of events that are meant to happen in future. We have been told that it is something that is totally beyond our control because we don't know what the future holds for us. But if we look closely, we will realise that we can control our future. How? By the decisions we make today. If we are mindful of our decisions today, we will see them making our tomorrow better. It is something as simple as deciding to be fit and healthy and then being rewarded with good health later.

My friend, life is too short to sit in the background and let everything pass by. While many things are beyond our control, a major part of our destiny is in our control. The good news is that at any moment, from this day forward, you can make a different choice and let it determine your future. So, what life-changing choice are you going to make today?

IT'S OKAY TO GO
Slow!

It's okay to go slow!

There is something we all have in common from our childhood—reading the 'Tortoise and the Rabbit' story. We all know how the rabbit was confident that it would win, but the tortoise won the race, slowly and steadily. Life seems like a race when everyone around us is trying to overtake someone. In this race, we are defined by our successes and looked down upon because of our failures. But we need to learn from the tortoise how to take it slow and not let the competition influence us.

Having said that, it isn't easy to slow down when everyone around you is rushing. We fear being left behind and losing the imaginary race that we are in. But the truth is that there is no fun or happiness being in a mindless rush that makes us live in anticipation of the future while ignoring the present. To appreciate the present, we must be mindful of our days, and to be mindful of our days, we must slow down.

And if you want to take it slow, let no one tell you otherwise. If the fear of being left behind worries you, disconnect yourself from the competition and breathe. The race exists just in our heads, anyway!

WAKE UP WITH A
thankful Heart!

Wake up with a thankful heart!

If the first thing you do after waking up in the morning is to check your phone, then you are not alone. If you wake up to the sound of notifications and not birds, then you are not alone. The fact is that this has become a daily lifestyle for so many people these days. We wake up and are bombarded with work emails, social media updates, and negative news from all corners. All of this stops us from giving our morning the kickstart it deserves.

But is there an ideal way of waking up in the morning? Yes, there is. Every day you wake up, you should show your gratitude and be thankful for the life you live, for the friends and family you have, and for the food you eat. And most importantly, you should be thankful for being alive. This will set the tone for the day. It will fill your heart with gratitude and make you look at the bright side of life. It will also make you look forward to what the day has in store for you with an optimistic approach.

So, if you want to make your days more beautiful, make it a habit to wake up with a grateful heart and see the magic that follows later.

ALLOW ONLY
Good Vibes!

Allow only good vibes!

Unlock your phone right now and notice all the applications you have. Have you turned on the notifications for all of these apps? Hope not! But imagine if you had. How distracting it would be if we are constantly being disturbed by some or the other notification. Also, not every app makes us feel good and probably this is why we don't give them unlimited access to our lives.

If we compare this to life, we will find a similarity. When we give too much access to people, emotions, and things that drain us, we feel exhausted. On the other hand, when we only allow people, feelings, and things that charge us up, we feel uplifted. Remember that we have the power to decide what vibes we want in our life. So, if bad vibes knock on your door in the form of people who pull you down or emotions that make you feel empty, it is essential to lock the door tight and not to let them enter. Let's give unlimited access to only good vibes and turn off notifications for everything else.

YOU CAN HAVE
it all!
LOVE
STRENGTH
JOY
MONEY
SUCCESS
PURPOSE
PASSION

You can have it all!

Some things don't go hand in hand. However, that is not the case with life. Here you can have everything you want without sacrificing something in return. You can have a great relationship and a thriving career. You can be strong and kind. You can be passionate about your goals and about having a life full of joys. You can make as much money as you want without having to sacrifice the time you spend with your family.

Some of us find it hard to believe this because we are conditioned to believe otherwise. But the truth is that you can have it all. Everything that you dream of is yours to have and is destined to be yours. People around you will always tell you to settle with what you have and do not dream of more. It is important to turn a deaf ear to them as they don't realise the immensity and abundance of life.

However, to have it all, we must be prepared to give it our all; our time, dedication, willpower, hard work, and discipline. Nothing will walk up to us till we take a step towards it ourselves. So, if you are among the few who want to have it all, then be among the few who are ready to give their all.

YOU ARE EXTREMELY
intuitive!

You are extremely intuitive!

Imagine if we had some kind of an indicating tool with us that would tell us whether the thing we are about to do is right or wrong. How great it would be to have such a gadget? The fact is that we do have such a tool inside us, and it is called *gut instinct*. This instinct guides us in situations where we need guidance and a push, and also alerts us in cases where we need to be alerted and take a step back. It is a voice that knows more than us . . . a voice that knows what is right and what is wrong for us.

But sometimes, it is challenging to listen to this instinct when we are surrounded by noise and distractions. Therefore, it is essential to slow down, take a break from distractions, and build a connection with ourselves. By doing so, our instinct will be able to communicate with us in a manner that would be easy for us to decode and decipher.

So, let's give our thinking mind a break and listen to our intuition that never lies. Let's try to understand what it is trying to tell us and then do as it says.

BE ENOUGH FOR *yourself first!*

Be enough for yourself first!

Right from our childhood, we have been taught that a good person is someone who is good to others. So, in an attempt to be such a person, we spend so much of our lives catering to the needs of people around us. We spend our time and energy being a good child to our parents, a good sibling to our siblings, a good friend to our friends, and a good partner to the love of our life. We spend a significant amount of time trying to meet the expectations of people around us.

While being there for others is the purest form of love, we must not forget ourselves in the process. We must listen to our needs and be there for ourselves as well. How can we do that, you ask? By not comparing ourselves with others, by not seeking approval from others, and by giving ourselves the love we expect from others. And this won't happen overnight. Take as much time as you need to but just make sure that you do at least one thing for yourself every day.

Fall in love unapologetically with the person you see in the mirror and make that person love you back, too. You deserve the love that you so kindly offer to others.

TRUST
Life!

Trust life!

Trust the ups and downs of life and everything in between as well. Trust the victories and the failures. Trust the cakewalks and the challenges. Trust the complexity and the simplicity. Because all of these have a role to play, and you may not be able to decode it right now but one day you will.

Remember that nothing happens to you, my friend; it happens for you. Everything that you have gone through was destined to take place so that you become the person you are today. All those moments of despair that you faced were meant to help you bloom. So, embrace the growth that you experience and the hardships that were a part of the process.

Replace 'Why did it happen to me?' with 'I am sure it happened for a reason'. Trust life and the plan it has for you even if it doesn't make any sense to you at times and feels that it is going against your wishes. Believe that it wants nothing but the best for you and it understands you better than you understand yourself.

So, ride on my friend! Your journey is going to be a smooth one.

LET GO OF ALL *your Baggage!*

Let go of all your baggage!

Did you know that professional trekkers usually pack light for their long treks? This is because the lighter their backpacks are, the longer the distance they would be able to cover. Likewise, all of us are trekkers in this journey called life. But sometimes, we tend to fill our backpacks with things we don't need. We add unnecessary worry, regrets, and resentments to it. Eventually, our baggage becomes heavy and we find it hard to push through.

In order to allow life to take us places, it is important that we unload what we don't need. And to do so, we must first acknowledge the emotions that hold us back. Then the next step includes accepting these emotions and leaving no room for denial. This should be followed by practising to live in the present and forgiving the past version of others and ourselves. Lastly, we should understand that there is so much life left for us to live and so much beauty we have yet to witness. Realising this fact would allow us to shed all the unnecessary baggage.

Understand that life is continuously moving and it is not only beneficial for us to move forward but also necessary.

YOUR GUIDANCE IS
rooted in your faith!

Your guidance is rooted in your faith!

When we say we have full faith in something, we mean that we have a strong belief and trust in it. Now, if we put our faith in people or things, they might disappoint us in the long run. But if we put our faith in the universe, it will never leave our side. And the stronger our faith, the more guided and protected we will be.

But what does having faith in the universe actually imply? It means to have a stronger belief that everything is working out in our favour, that we are always looked after by a force stronger than us, and that we are loved and blessed forever. And when we develop this faith, we become like a tree with strong, deep roots that can't be shaken by the storms of life. With such anchored roots, the tree will be able to spread its branches and explore the infinite possibilities of life irrespective of the weather or changing seasons.

So, would you also like to be deeply rooted in life? If your answer is yes, then remind yourself that the universe is 'rooting' for you, both literally and metaphorically!

BE THE ENERGY
you want to attract!

Be the energy you want to attract!

Have you noticed that you feel happy and cheerful in the company of certain people while drained and insecure in the presence of others? This is because we all are made up of energy that vibrates around us. You must have also noticed how you prefer being around people who emit positive energy and avoid people who radiate negative energy. But do you know that we attract the energy we send into the universe? Maybe this is why when we are having a bad day, everything around us tends to make it even worse. It now makes sense, right?

Therefore, we should ensure that the energy we give out to the universe is the same energy we want to attract. Meaning, if we want to be appreciated, then we should appreciate everyone and everything around us. If we want to be loved, we should treat everyone around us with love. If we want to be understood, we should try to understand people around us. And then we will see the magic of this energy. We will see it coming back to us in ways we never even imagined!

FACE EVERYTHING
& Rise!

Face everything & rise!

We all have faced some kind of fear in our lives. It is an inevitable part of life. And when we come across an uncertain and frightening situation, our default instinct is to become paranoid about what might happen. Such scary situations trigger the psychological alarm inside us, which makes us even more tense and worried.

But there is a way we can get rid of fear. Zig Ziglar, an American author and a motivational speaker, once said, "F-E-A-R has two meanings: Forget Everything and Run or Face Everything and Rise. The choice is yours." This choice is indeed ours. If we choose the former definition, we hide away from the lessons that fear can possibly teach us. But if we choose the latter, we can face our fears head on and make use of them as stepping stones to something better.

Take a moment to think of your first job. In the beginning, you might not have been that good at your work but must have gradually improved. This is what experience does to us. It increases our knowledge and makes us stronger and more prepared. The experience of fear, once faced, does the same. Those who choose to run away from this fear, choose to run away from the experience. By the way, running of this kind doesn't even help us burn any calories! So, what's the point?

THE UNIVERSE IS ALWAYS
supporting you!

The universe is always supporting you!

We all want a friend who would be there for us when life gets tough . . . a friend who would support us, no matter what our dreams or aspiration might be. The truth is that the universe meets all these requirements and more. Thus, if we befriend the universe and truly put our faith in it, it will never betray us. It will become our greatest cheerleader, our pillar of strength, and a powerful force always ready to back us up. And when life would demand us to take a decision, it will guide us in the form of intuition. And when life would want us to reach our highest potential, it will give us the power and determination to achieve it.

All we need to do is let go of our fears and put our complete faith in the universe. So, the next time you are worried about falling, remind yourself that the universe and the floor will always have your back.

TREAT
yourself!

Treat yourself!

Juggling work and personal life isn't an easy task. It requires us to be constantly on our toes in order to manage the never-ending responsibilities. And it is commendable the way you still manage to give a bit of your time and energy to people when they need you. The truth is that even though there is so much that you do every day, you give yourself so little credit for it. You might think that there is nothing extraordinary about you managing all aspects of life like a pro, but I beg to differ. I believe that you outdo yourself every single day and for that, you must be celebrated.

But should we always rely on others to celebrate ourselves? No, we shouldn't. Given below are some ways you can celebrate yourself:

1. Identify what sparks a light within you and do more of it.
2. Reconnect with your childhood friends. They always help us look back and acknowledge how far we have come.
3. Engage in activities that are good for your mind, body, and soul.
4. Learn something new that your future self will thank you for.
5. Take a day off from everything and do nothing.
6. Declutter your space.
7. Hug yourself for making it this far.

Now that you know why it is important to celebrate yourself, make sure that it becomes a part of your lifestyle!

ASK AND IT IS, *Given!*

Ask and it is given!

Communication is a vital part of any kind of relationship. Every relationship has its share of ups and downs, but communication can make the ups better and help survive the downs. A lot of times, we expect people to understand us without communicating our needs to them. But this is wrong because for our needs to be truly met, we must learn to communicate properly.

Similarly, when it comes to having a meaningful relationship with the universe, communication plays a significant role here as well. We must learn to communicate with the universe and listen to its answers which we receive in the form of signs and intuition. In order to receive what we desire and wish to achieve, we must learn to ask. But before asking, we must be clear about our desires and why we want what we want. Once we are clear about our desires, we must ensure that our intentions are pure and then ask the universe to manifest them. The universe will listen to our desires and work towards making our wishes come true. And with some visualisation and emission of positive energy, we will be able to get all that we truly want.

And remember that the best part about having a relationship with the universe is that it doesn't panic when you say, "We need to talk!"

ENJOY THE RIDE
of Life!

Enjoy the ride of life!

What can we say about the low points of life? They bring with them nothing but misery and pain. And it takes years for us to get over them. So what if they teach us some valuable lessons? We don't want any experience that teaches us lessons but makes our heart hurt and eyes shed an ocean of tears. Why can't our life be full of highs, one accompanied by the other? Wouldn't it be marvellous, we often think to ourselves.

But rarely do we realise that it is these lows that make the highs far more enjoyable and cherished. Just like only when we spend a significant time in the dark do we appreciate the light; in a similar manner, only when we experience sadness do we realise what it means to be truly happy.

Enjoy the moments of laughter and the opportunities that help you rise. But also come to terms with the grief that comes your way. So, learn to release your emotions instead of suppressing them. Try talking to someone you trust and can confide in. Practise mindfulness and always keep the spark of hope in you alive and see how it will work as a seat belt in this roller coaster of life. It will guard you, protect you, and help you get through the lows.

YOUR DREAMS WILL
come true!

Your dreams will come true!

Dreams are private possessions. No one can ever take them away from us. We spend hours daydreaming about achieving them without a tinge of regret. And to top it all, we have a relentless drive to achieve them.

If you too have a dream, allow me to take a moment to let you know that it will come true. The universe observes the passion you work with to achieve your dream. It notices your dedication, your discipline, and your intentions and conspires everything to work in your favour.

You are going to witness the magic soon. Your desires are about to be manifested into reality and it is going to be even better than how you envisioned it. Make space for it in your life and feed this dream with the love it deserves. Visualise achieving it and act as if you already have. Let this be a warm-up for what is about to take place.

EVERYTHING COMES TO YOU
at the right time!

Everything comes to you at the right time!

Everything comes to you at the right time. This line might not make sense to you right now, especially if you are desperately wanting to have something for a long time, but eventually, it will.

While we think we are powerful enough to make our decisions, there is a force that is more powerful than us and it has planned everything for us. Every single episode that we go through in our life is consciously planned by this force to serve its purpose. We might get anxious and stress over our desires, spending days and months obsessing over them. But the important thing to realise is that they will come to us only when the time is right.

Put your faith in the divine timing of the universe which is continuously working to fulfil our desires. But to fully believe this, there are some things that we must do:

1. Let go of control. Learn to unclench your wrist every now and then and let go of the need to control your life.
2. There is a force that is competent enough to take care of you and your life. Surrender yourself to that force.
3. Lastly, learn to be patient. Stop yourself from rushing into things and instead, be patient to witness what the universe has planned for you.

Bring all of these points to execution and see the difference. Know that life has a plan for you and it will all make sense in the end. Life doesn't work any other way, dear.

STAY
Grateful!

Stay grateful!

It is hard to look at the bright side of life when we are stuck in a difficult situation. And I won't sugarcoat this fact and tell you things like that life is a cakewalk and everything is easy. Instead, I will be blunt and tell you that life can truly be hard at times and it is not an easy ride on many days.

But having said that, I deeply believe that even on the darkest days, one can turn on the light by being grateful. But the question is how can one be grateful? The answer lies in detaching ourselves from the shoulds and coulds and accepting things and situations as they are. We can also be grateful by accepting our past gracefully, not stressing over the future, and living mindfully in the present.

Religious and spiritual teachings also talk about exploring gratitude and say that it is a way to thank the higher power. The truth is that the benefits of being grateful are immense, both physically as well as psychologically. It makes us optimistic and happier and helps improve the quality of life and overall health. It also helps control our negative emotions and makes us more likeable as human beings.

Here is a fun gratitude activity for you. Make a gratitude jar, decorate it with all things beautiful, and every time something good happens, write it on a piece of paper and put it in the jar. And whenever you feel a little low in life, take these pieces of paper out of the jar and revisit the good times. They will fill your heart with joy and instantly cheer you up.

BELIEVE

in yourself!

Believe in yourself!

Every time you look at yourself in the mirror, do you notice all the minute details that make you? The texture of your skin, the colour of your eyes, the shape of your eyebrows, and the way your lips form a curved moon when you smile. Do you ever take notice of how your every single feature is so uniquely different from that of others?

The reason why so much detailing has gone into making us is that we are loved by this universe. This, in itself, should make us believe in ourselves and convince us that we are among the chosen ones who get to experience the immensity of life. This trait of believing in oneself is a common thread among many successful people. This belief gives them the courage to overcome all obstacles and pushes them to work hard in order to achieve their goals. We, too, need to trust ourselves and have faith in our skills and strengths. By doing so, we can give ourselves the push we need to achieve our goals and the confidence to face every challenge head-on.

So, are you ready to reward yourself with the greatest gift . . . the gift of believing in yourself?

END THE DAY WITH A
Positive thought!

End the day with a positive thought!

Imagine it is 11 o'clock in the night. You have had a scrumptious dinner followed by a light conversation with your family. You go for a little walk and then decide to hop into the bed. Suddenly your mind starts to wander and you start thinking about your friends, your colleagues, and life in general. Some of this remembrance evokes positive feelings in you while some parts of it evoke not so positive feelings. And before you know, you are asleep.

This scenario is a reality for a lot of us. We spend our days mindlessly waiting for the hour hand of the clock to reach six, after which we will watch something that will take our mind off from all that is happening around us, and then we will finally reach out to our pillows for a good sleep. But this is not how our day should end. Every single day of our lives should instead end on a positive note. We must look back at our day and absorb the positivity it added to our lives while letting go of the not so good moments. Keep a gratitude journal on your bedside table and make it a habit to revisit your blessings each night and add them to your journal. This will not only help you sleep better and wake up rejuvenated the next day but it will also ensure that you become more positive day by day.

So, from today, before you hit the bed, think of a thought that uplifts you. It could be something that someone said, something that made you laugh or smile, or it could simply be something that you are grateful for. Practice it every day and see how your life changes, one night at a time.

DREAM WITHOUT
Fear!

Dream without fear!

If you ask children what they want to be when they grow up, they would instantly and proudly tell you their most prominent dream. It could be to become an astronomer, a scientist, a pilot, an artist, or a doctor. They don't fear being judged, questioned, or laughed upon. They dare to dream without these fears. But as we grow up, the limitless sky of our childhood starts to shrink and our dreams, more often than not, begin to be defined by our fears.

In order to live a fulfilled life, we must find that childlike innocence again and dream without fears and apprehensions. We must dream as if everything that we want is ours to have. And then miracles will start to happen. Remember that no matter how big or small, every dream of ours will find its way to us and become a part of our reality.

So, let's refrain from letting our fears define our dreams and thinking that any dream is unachievable. Let's dream because that is where it all starts. It is the first step towards living an extraordinary life, and who doesn't want that!

HANG IN
there!

Hang in there!

We can all agree that life gets a little messy sometimes. During such times, we try our best to attain our goals and keep ourselves on track but nothing seems to work out in our favour. It is in these times that we find ourselves second-guessing if we should actually continue to pursue our goals. Putting our goals on hold and giving up seems like the only sane thing to do when we are stuck in a rut. But giving up after working relentlessly towards our goals is like trying to open a jar of pickles and quitting right before the moment it was about to open. By doing so, not only do our efforts go to waste, but we also deprive ourselves of experiencing success.

Hope is what we need to give ourselves to get us through these challenging moments. We should remind ourselves that there is something good on the other side of the struggle and that we will witness it very soon if we just hang in there. And no matter how tough it gets, giving up should never be on our to-do list.

So, folks never-ever give up on anything . . . not even when it feels impossible to open a jar of pickles!

THE ART OF
Letting Go!

The art of letting go!

Every new chapter of our life demands us to close an old one. However, sometimes it is not as easy as it sounds and we can't help but have one foot in the past. And by clinging on to the past, we stop ourselves from completely exploring the present and seeing the beauty in it.

What we need to realise is that holding on to what is gone does nothing but only causes more suffering. This is why we must learn to let go. Here are some ways to do so:

1. Change the way you talk about your past. Instead of saying 'that relationship broke me', substitute it with 'that relationship made me realise what I deserve'.
2. When your mind starts to wander, try to bring it back to the present moment.
3. Be gentle with yourself. Don't punish yourself for feeling what you feel. Give yourself time and space to heal.
4. Learn to forgive. Don't wait for someone to apologise to you. By doing this, you give them the power to control your life.
5. Some experiences are way too hurtful to let go of. If you have had such an experience, seek professional help.

There is an additional exercise that I would like to share with you. Make a list of all the things that you need to let go of. Everything that no longer serves you. And read them out loud after prefixing them with 'I let you go'.

BE STRONGER
than your excuses!

Be stronger than your excuses!

Excuses are like empty vessels that just make noise. And at times, they are so loud that we fail to listen to our heart or our rational mind. To succumb to them is to settle for something far less than what we deserve and nobody wants that.

This is why it is important to be stronger than our excuses and not let them dominate our choices and actions. The first step to ensure the same is by identifying if something is an excuse or a valid reason. Every time you find yourself contemplating some matter, try to understand if there is truly a reason behind it or is just an excuse. If it turns out to be the latter, learn to ignore it.

Now, if you are someone who finds it hard to stay focused and committed to your goals, you can try Mel Robbins' the 5 Second Rule. This rule suggests that when we have an instinct to act on a goal, we must physically move within 5 seconds or our brain will kill it. Thus, it is important to immediately get up and get going before your thoughts convince you otherwise. Ignore the irrational thoughts and listen to what your gut is trying to speak to you. Be bigger than the voice in your head and what society tells you.

So, never let your excuses stop you from becoming a better version of yourself and achieving your goals.

DELETE *Negativity!*

Delete negativity!

Negativity is like mist on a pair of spectacles. It distorts our vision and makes life look less beautiful. Not only this, but it also affects our health, our well-being, and even our minds.

Eliminating negativity is not easy but certainly not impossible. But what are the steps to get rid of draining emotions that walk into our lives and try to reside there permanently? The first thing to realise is that while negativity might arise out of both external and internal reasons, in order to combat it, we must start from inside. This includes not considering every thought as a fact. Just because your mind says something, doesn't mean it is necessarily true.

Now coming to the external factors. Sometimes people around us add a dose of negativity to our lives. They can do so by doing or saying something that triggers negative emotions. So, if you have a friend who always pulls you down or a relative who always compares you with someone else or if there is someone on social media who makes you love yourself less, unfollow them from your real a well as digital life. This would help to keep the source of negativity at bay. And if the mist still fogs up your glasses, use some positive affirmations to wipe it away.

YOUR MIND
is limitless!

Your mind is limitless!

Don't we all wish for a magic wand with which we can create a world of our dreams? A wand that lets us attain a fulfilling and happy life. But what most of us don't know is that we already possess a magic wand. Yes, we do and that magic wand is our mind. Our mind has the capability to open doors to infinite possibilities. It can do so by visualisation which is the first step towards creating a reality. With the limitless power of our mind and some faith in the universe, we can create a world we truly desire.

However, this magic wand comes with some drawbacks too. If not controlled properly, it can create a world that doesn't align with the world of our dreams. Hence, it is crucial that we learn to control it. And once we are able to control our mind, we can control our thoughts, and when we can control our thoughts, we can unlock the true power of visualisation and create our dream world.

So, let's put this magic wand to good use and create a beautiful life for ourselves and everyone else!

LEARN ABOUT Yourself!

Learn about yourself!

Every phase of life involves meeting new people, and in order to become friends with them, we try to learn more about them. We ask them about their favourite show, their favourite food, their favourite place to hang out in the city, and more. This is how we bond with them. But rarely do we try to learn more about ourselves or make an effort to build a bond with ourselves. Maybe because we seldom feel the need to do so. However, this leads to missing out on the chance to befriend ourselves . . . the only person who will never leave our side. And what a loss that is!

Don't let this happen. Do better and ask yourself questions you would ask a potential friend. Learn about your strengths, your weaknesses, your insecurities, your fears. Learn about what makes you happy, what makes you sad, and what you truly want out of your life. Learn all this and more till you know who you indeed are. Don't deprive yourself of this joy.

So, make sure that the next date that you go on is with the person you have within yourself.

NO RAINBOW
without Rain!

No rainbow without rain!

We all know that the tree or plant on which our favourite fruit grows was once a seed. Someone had to sow that seed, give it water and fertilisers, ensure that it got proper sunlight, and look after it almost every day. Not only this, but it also requires a lot of patience from the person growing the tree/plant. Such people know that to enjoy the fruit, they will have to go through some hardships as well.

Similarly, our goals demand our attention, discipline, hard work, undying determination, and a positive outlook. Once we feed them all of this and are patient enough to see the final results, only then they become our reality. Experiencing some hardships along the way is just part of the process. They make our journey worthwhile as, without them, it will be an easy ride lacking all kinds of thrills and excitement. Someone has rightly said that if achieving your goals is easy, then your goals are not big enough. There needs to be some challenge because only when we go through challenges, there is a possibility for personal growth.

Therefore, we must be accepting of the challenges and rains we face on our journey because they help us experience successes and rainbows. Remember that for a rainbow to appear, rain is necessary!

LEARN TO APPRECIATE
what you have!

Learn to appreciate what you have!

As human beings, we tend to appreciate the past and the future but not what we currently have. During summers, we crib over the heat and wish for winters to come early. And during winters, we fret about wearing too many clothes and wish for summers to begin already. This holds true for many other areas of our life as well. We often take the little joys for granted, like taking our dog for a walk, living with our families, having someone to call our own, and so on. This happens primarily due to our never-ending pursuit of a bigger bliss.

That is the thing about our desires; they make everything else look small in front of them. Rarely do we appreciate the things we have, even if at some point, those things were all that we wanted. However, to appreciate life and the beauty around us, we must first appreciate what we have. If finding contentment in life is our goal, then we must practise gratitude and thank the universe for everything we have. Not only will it make us more humble but also attract more happy moments in our lives. And I am sure we all can use some extra happiness!

DO GOOD AND
good will come to you!

Do good and good will come to you!

To withdraw money from an ATM, we enter the amount we wish to withdraw, and then the ATM machine obliges to our request. Life is like an ATM of goodness. It expects us to enter goodness into it to give us the same in return. The world calls this *karma* which means that everyone in the world will reap what they sow. Meaning, our actions today will determine our tomorrow.

But should we only do good to get goodness in return? No! We should do good because we want to do good. We should do good because the world needs good. We should do good, not for a cause but for the effect it will have on us, on the people around us, and on the world as a whole.

Now, let's discuss how this goodness comes back to us. Sometimes, it happens immediately— we help someone and they feel happy, which in turn makes us feel happy. Sometimes, it can come out of nowhere and when we least expect it. This goodness can come in any form of love, kindness, and generosity when it is needed the most. If it takes a little longer than usual, hold on and don't lose hope. Be sure that the ATM of goodness has some goodness inside it for everybody. And when the time is right, it will come to you!

MAKE YOUR VISION
crystal clear!

Make your vision crystal clear!

Whenever we visit a tailor to get something stitched, we make sure to provide them with all the necessary details—what particular fabric to use, the outfit's colour, the design/style we are interested in, etc. We go into every last single detail concerning the outfit because we want to ensure that the final result is precisely how we have envisioned it.

Similarly, when it comes to our life's vision, we should get into the same kind of detailing or maybe even more. We should be clear about the life we desire, the goals—both short-term and long-term—we want to achieve, and the potential obstacles we could face while working towards these goals. Having a clear vision will help you discover the path towards this vision. It will also remove every possible distraction and help you put your heart and soul towards achieving your vision.

So, even if your idea of an ideal life involves having a tub of ice cream every day, be crystal clear about it!

THANK YOU
Universe!

Thank you universe!

We are immensely thankful for friends who always stand by our side and we show our gratitude to them in different ways. But there is one more important friend that we need to add to that list—the universe. It not only supports our dreams and ambitions but also makes sure that we are happy. It manifests our dreams into actual realities and blesses us with an abundance of everything that is good. Know that the universe is our biggest cheerleader!

So, should you think twice before thanking this friend? No, never! Thanking the universe for everything that it does for us will ensure that we attract more of its blessings into our lives. It is only a matter of showing our appreciation for all the gifts life has showered on us.

So today, let us show our gratitude to the universe for all the opportunities we receive, all the success that comes our way, and for the moments that make our life worthwhile. We can do so by including positive statements like 'I am grateful for everything you have done for me', 'I am thankful to you for always ensuring the best for me', and 'I am thankful for the life you have given me'. The universe will then accept our token of gratitude and give us more reasons to be thankful about. Remember to keep this in your thoughts and prayers every single day.

LET THE UNIVERSE
direct your steps!

Let the universe direct your steps!

Everything in your life seems to be going well. You have a decent job that pays you well, a family that loves you, and friends who are always there for you. But still, sometimes you wonder if there is a life beyond all this, if there is a bigger purpose for you, and if you will ever achieve the silent dreams that you have. The dreams that you don't talk to anyone about because they seem to be too good to be true and you fear people will judge you.

Today, on the behalf of the universe, I want to ascertain that you will soon achieve those dreams and everything that is happening with you right now is just a part of the process. You don't see it but the universe has been guiding you all along, giving you signs, and sometimes even speaking to you in the form of your intuition. And it will continue to do so forever. It knows your deepest desires and is conspiring everything so that they become your reality one day.

So, give yourself a minute today to breathe and trust the grand plan. Tell the universe that you trust it and see where it takes you.

ACKNOWLEDGEMENTS

The Little Book of Good Things! could not have come into the world without the help and support of many.

First, I wish to acknowledge and thank the universe for everything.

A special thanks to my husband, Honey, for all the love and support that has made me who I am today. For all the times you wiped my tears, hugged me tight, watched me fail, helped me succeed . . . this is for you.

I have immense cuddle-filled gratitude for my pet, Fudge, without whom my life would have been different. Thank you for your love, warmth, and uncountable licks.

Thank you to my mommy and daddy in heaven for raising me well, always blessing and supporting me, making me strong, and loving me for who I am, no matter the realm. I hope I will continue to make you proud!

To the members of The Doodle Desk team who worked with me on *The Little Book of Good Things!*, especially Manisha. There are no words that can describe my gratitude for your dedication and support. You are indeed our Sunflower!

Many thanks to my friends who are also my family, especially Akshata, Gurpreet, Japun, Mital, Mukta, Ruchi, and Sargam, for all the encouragement you all gave through my tough times and for being my guiding light when I was in utmost darkness. I am indeed so blessed to have you all in my life. I love you all.

My utmost gratitude to Rohini Singh. Aunty, you are my angel!

Thank you to the most amazing team of Hay House India. You all were such a joy to work with. Thank you for bringing my dream to life!

And as always, a special thank you to my virtual family that has supported my art and has rooted for me all these years. Thank you for believing in me, loving me, and being my biggest support system. This book would not have been possible without you all.

Lastly, I would like to express my deep gratitude to my teacher, Shiva.

Scan me for
daily motivation

Daily Ü

ABOUT THE AUTHOR

Bhavya Doshi is an artist, an entrepreneur, and a visual-based motivational producer. Being a 40 under 40 positively influential social-media superstar and a role player recognised by the World Marketing Congress, Bhavya believes in 'the art of spreading joy'. Art has been a getaway for her since childhood but became a coping mechanism when she lost both her parents. She explored multiple roles in the corporate world, but nothing made her as happy as creating art. In 2018, she took a paradigm leap in her career and focused on pursuing her love for art full-time and eventually thought of starting a mental-health and self-motivation platform to help others. That is how The Doodle Desk came to life and it has now become an attestation of hope and a minimalistic, unique, and colourful stress-management pitstop for people.

Bhavya believes that art can change the world, and she uses it to inspire and empower people of all age groups by designing cute minimal illustrations, each with a strong positive message. She now aims to continue to touch the lives of people in more ways than one. Hence, *The Little Book of Good Things!*

You can connect with her on Instagram @thedoodledesk. If you wish to receive your daily dose of inspiration from The Doodle Desk, visit thedoodledesk.com.